# JUMPIN' JIM's®
## *Gone* HOLLYWOOD

### Compiled And Arranged By Jim Beloff

T0040748

## *The Songs*

Silent screen actress, Dorothy Gulliver

Copyright © 2003 FLEA MARKET MUSIC, INC.

**HAL•LEONARD®**
**CORPORATION**
7777 W. BLUEMOUND RD. P.O. BOX 13819 MILWAUKEE, WI 53213

Edited by Ronny S. Schiff
Cover and Art Direction by Elizabeth Maihock Beloff
Graphics and Music Typography by Charylu Roberts

# FOREWORD

 ights! Camera! Action! Ukuleles! So many wonderful songs have been introduced in motion pictures that it seemed only natural to pull together some of the best for this songbook. As with our other books, one essential criterion for a song's inclusion is whether it sounds good strummed on a ukulele. Not surprisingly, the older songs like "Singin' In The Rain" and others from that period were the most appealing. Written when the ukulele was a part of the popular culture, these songs are served well by a strummed accompaniment. As a result, this book leans heavily on songs from movies made during the '30s through the '60s.

That being said, we couldn't help including a few of those wonderfully lush, sweeping movie themes. Songs like, "The Shadow Of Your Smile" and "What Are You Doing The Rest Of Your Life?" require rich, jazz chords, but, with some practice, can sound just as rich and beautiful on a ukulele.

It was a real treat and honor to have the noted film critic and historian, Leonard Maltin, write the appreciation this time. His deep passion for film, music, Hawaii and, of course, ukuleles was a great source of inspiration. He was also a big help in assembling the "Ukuleles In The Movies" feature. This section grew out of a smaller one started in *The Ukulele: A Visual History.*

As always there are many hands that help shape these songbooks. First and foremost, a big thank you to my wife and partner, Liz Beloff, who art directs all of our songbooks. Thanks also to Jeanine Basinger, Peter Bateman, Doug, Dorathy and Hartley Haverty, Mimi Kennedy, Leonard and Alice Maltin, Carl Reiner, Peter Wingerd and Judy Wolman. Additional photos and sheet music courtesy of Jim Duron, Ewa Noskowicz and Geoff Rezek. And, as always, many thanks to Charylu Roberts and Ronny Schiff for doing what you do. Thanks for the memory!

—Jumpin' Jim Beloff

**Also Available: (Books)** *Jumpin' Jim's Ukulele Favorites; Jumpin' Jim's Ukulele Tips 'n' Tunes; Jumpin' Jim's Ukulele Gems; Jumpin' Jim's Ukulele Christmas; Jumpin' Jim's '60s Uke-In; Jumpin' Jim's Gone Hawaiian; Jumpin' Jim's Camp Ukulele; Jumpin' Jim's Ukulele Masters: Lyle Ritz; Jumpin' Jim's Ukulele Beach Party; Jumpin' Jim's Ukulele Masters: Herb Ohta; Jumpin' Jim's Ukulele Masters: Lyle Ritz Solos; Jumpin' Jim's Ukulele Spirit; The Ukulele: A Visual History.* **(CDs)** *Jim's Dog Has Fleas; For The Love Of Uke; Legends Of Ukulele; It's A Fluke; Lyle Ritz & Herb Ohta—A Night Of Ukulele Jazz.* **(Video)** *The Joy Of Uke.*

Visit us on the web at www.fleamarketmusic.com

# LEONARD MALTIN
## On Ukuleles

I suppose it's natural that because I love old movies, I also love the ukulele. The uke was such a familiar fixture in American life during the 1920s and '30s that it naturally turned up in a great many movies. As a collector of movie-related sheet music of the period, I also learned a long time ago that virtually all printed copies of my favorite songs came complete with ukulele chords.

Jim Beloff, the Johnny Appleseed of the uke, has chosen a wonderful variety of songs for this collection, based on their connection to movies. In some cases the choices are obvious; others, like "What Are You Doing The Rest Of Your Life?" and "The Shadow Of Your Smile" may seem a bit of a stretch, but believe me, they sound great if you sing and strum them with the proper approach.

Some of the most durable songs in this assemblage have a strong connection to the uke, because they were first performed by the great Cliff "Ukulele Ike" Edwards. Edwards is a hero to all true ukulele fans, and it's said that his 1924 recording of "June Night" was the first million-selling record in history. Cliff was strumming away when he introduced "Singin' In The Rain" in *The Hollywood Revue Of 1929*, and scored another hit with "It's Only A Paper Moon" in the little-remembered 1933 musical *Take A Chance*. (This adaptation of the Broadway hit also included my favorite Edwards number, too obscure for this anthology but worth checking out: "Night Owl.")

But even people who can't muster up a mental picture of Cliff Edwards know him as the voice of Jiminy Cricket in *Pinocchio*, and it was in that film that he introduced the Oscar-winning song that went on to become the Disney anthem, "When You Wish Upon A Star."

You'll surely know a lot of the songs in these pages, which makes them fun to sing, alone or with a group of like-minded friends. But I can take credit for introducing Jumpin' Jim to one obscure number that we both fell in love with, because it's performed so endearingly by Gracie Allen—and her uke—in the 1939 MGM musical *Honolulu*. I think you'll like it, if you give it a try.

My family and I have been inspired to take up the ukulele in recent years, and I wish I could say that we've mastered the instrument, but I can join the growing number of enthusiasts who have learned how much fun it is to play, especially in a group. I hope that our society of True Believers will increase when other old-movie buffs latch on to this book.

*Leonard Maltin*

Leonard Maltin is best known as the film critic and historian for television's *Entertainment Tonight*, and as the co-host of the weekly movie review show *Hot Ticket*. He is also the author of many books and articles about film, and edits the annual paperback reference *Leonard Maltin's Movie & Video Guide*.

# UKULELES *In The* MOVIES

For many fans of the ukulele, any pop culture visibility of the instrument is worth noting. Today, a current film that includes a uke is a positive sign. Of course, during the heyday years it wasn't odd at all to see ukuleles in movies. This was even more the case in older movies set in Hawaii or on college campuses.

Probably the two most memorable movies to include ukes are *Blue Hawaii* where Elvis strums and *Some Like It Hot* where Marilyn Monroe does the same. Over the years, we've seen or heard of other movies that include uke scenes. It is probably unrealistic to identify every movie made that includes a uke, but our attempt here was to verify and acknowledge many of the most important ones.

There is one other point worth underscoring: Often the poster or photo still of an older movie set in Hawaii, or in a college, features a character holding a ukulele. As a result, one would think that a uke was featured in that film. In reality, this turned out to be an unreliable clue. In these cases the uke was just a prop used to help sell the implied "island-ness" or "merriment" of the picture.

*A Connecticut Yankee In King Arthur's Court*, 1949. Paramount Pictures. Bing Crosby teaches King Arthur's court musicians to swing. As he re-tunes one fellow's uke-like instrument, Crosby says, "There's a new tuning on these instruments, gonna sweep the country." After tuning up to the "my-dog-has-fleas" tuning, Crosby states, "There's a canoe that goes with these things, but that's another story."

*Blue Hawaii,* 1961. Paramount Pictures. This was Elvis Presley's biggest box-office hit and the soundtrack recording to the film (featuring Presley playing the uke on the cover) was his thirteenth Gold Record. The soundtrack recording was also Presley's longest-running Number One album on the *Billboard* charts, lasting a total of 20 weeks.

*The Caine Mutiny,* 1954. Columbia Pictures. Brief scene where a junior officer on the Caine strums and sings "I've got those yellow stain blues..." referring to Humphrey Bogart's earlier cowardly action.

Joan Blackman and Elvis Presley in *Blue Hawaii*. Hal Wallis Productions/ Paramount Pictures, 1962.

*The Glass Bottom Boat,* 1966. MGM. A comic romp set on Catalina Island. Arthur Godfrey plays Doris Day's father and in the middle of the picture plays a cutaway baritone, while Day sings the title tune and a chorus of her big hit "Que Sera, Sera."

*Go For Broke,* 1951. MGM. Van Johnson leads the 442nd regiment, a unit of Japanese American soldiers and Hawaiians during World War II. One Hawaiian soldier in the unit strums his uke throughout the entire film. While stationed in Europe, he is delighted to receive two packs of uke strings in the mail.

*Good News,* 1947. MGM. A young Mel Tormé strums and sings "Lucky In Love" on what looks like a Martin concert. It appears that Mel is actually playing the uke, which supports the story that later on he used the four strings of a uke to help him write big band arrangements.

*Hawaii Calls*, 1938. RKO. Bobby Breen stars as a young stowaway headed for Hawaii in this musical comedy/drama. Ukes are visible in most of the musical numbers and there is some great uke-centered dialogue. Early in the film, a ship's steward asks Ned Sparks to get him a uke when they get to Honolulu. Sparks refuses saying, "...there are too many ukulele players in the world, now." When they find a scratching dog on-board ship, Breen and his Hawaiian friend Pua name him Ukulele, for his "jumping fleas."

Bobby Breen and "Ukie" in *Hawaii Calls*. RKO, 1938.

*The Hollywood Revue Of 1929*, 1929. MGM. This early film is notable for Cliff Edwards' (Ukulele Ike) introduction of "Singin' In The Rain." He appears earlier in the film and performs "Nobody But You" with the entire chorus strumming on prop ukes. Bessie Love also appears and strums.

*Honolulu*, 1939. MGM. Gracie Allen strums a ukulele and sings the title tune. While tuning her uke, she admits to Eleanor Powell, "You see what's wrong, ...the dogs are all right, but the fleas are out of tune."

*The Hudsucker Proxy*, 1994. Warner Bros. Typically off-center Coen Brothers film about big business shenanigans. At the end of the film, Charles Durning appears dressed as an angel, strumming a uke and singing "She'll Be Coming 'Round The Mountain."

*The Jerk*, 1979. Universal Pictures. Great scene where Steve Martin strums a uke and sings "Tonight You Belong To Me" with Bernadette Peters. The dubbed uke playing was provided by the great jazz uke virtuoso, Lyle Ritz. According to director, Carl Reiner, they filmed this scene in Paradise Cove (California) at three in the morning. Steve Martin stepped on the only uke they had. At first, Reiner was thinking of running back to Beverly Hills to get his wife's (Estelle) Martin uke, but it was going to take an hour each way. Instead, the prop master traced the front of a uke on a clipboard, cut out the shape and glued that onto the broken uke that was used. No sound came from it, but it worked fine as a prop.

*Joe Versus The Volcano*, 1990. Warner Bros. Tom Hanks appears to be playing an early Martin 3M. Hanks picks a bit in several scenes, and then he strums and sings "The Cowboy Song," while floating on his luggage in the middle of the ocean.

*Love Affair*, 1939. RKO. Irene Dunne strums a uke in this classic film. She leads a group of children in the beautiful song, "Wishing."

Jessica Harper, Bernadette Peters and Steve Martin in *Pennies From Heaven*. MGM, 1981.

*Marianne*, 1929. MGM. This World War I musical comedy stars Marion Davies as a French woman being wooed by an American soldier. Three songs are accompanied by a ukulele including two strummed by co-star, Cliff Edwards.

*Mixed Nuts*, 1994. TriStar. As one of the "nuts," Adam Sandler plays "Deck The Halls" on what appears to be a Martin 0.

*Pennies From Heaven*, 1981. MGM. Steve Martin plays a tenor uke during a performance of "Life Is Just A Bowl Of Cherries."

*Please Don't Eat The Daisies,* 1960. MGM. Doris Day sings and strums the title tune with a group of children.

*The Purple Rose Of Cairo*, 1985. Orion. Woody Allen gives the uke a supporting role in this wonderful movie. In front of a music store, Mia Farrow admits to Jeff Daniels that "I can play the ukulele. My father taught me before he ran away." Farrow then strums a very respectable "Alabamy Bound" on what looks like a Martin 0.

*Some Like It Hot,* 1959. United Artists. Marilyn Monroe plays musician/singer Sugar Kane in this Billy Wilder classic. Her painted white uke is featured in the production number "Runnin' Wild." One of the special treats of the soundtrack album is the famous Richard Avedon stills on the cover of Ms. Monroe cavorting with her uke.

*Sons Of The Desert,* 1933. MGM. Ollie plays the uke and sings "Honolulu Baby" in this classic Laurel and Hardy misadventure.

*Stage Door,* 1937. RKO. Scene with Ginger Rogers strumming a uke. Looks and sounds like she is really playing the chords to "Five Foot Two, Eyes Of Blue." At one point someone tries to grab her uke whereupon she says, "You're interfering with my art."

Laurel and Hardy in
*Sons Of The Desert*. MGM, 1933.

*Stanley's Gig,* 2001. Left Hook Productions. Uke-playing William Sanderson (Stanley) meets reclusive, former jazz singer, Marla Gibbs while entertaining at a retirement home. Through his efforts, he helps her to reconcile with her past. Features a final concert starring Stanley and his uke. The film includes a number of fine songs written, sung and strummed by Ian Whitcomb.

*A Thousand Clowns,* 1965. United Artists. Eccentric uncle, Jason Robards and nephew, Barry Gordon, both strum and sing "Yes, Sir, That's My Baby."

*Tin Pan Alley,* 1940. Twentieth Century-Fox. Alice Faye and Betty Grable strum all-white ukuleles in this film about a couple of struggling songwriters. In a running gag throughout the movie, they sing dummy lyrics to what eventually becomes the song, "K-K-K-Katy." Their "Hawaiian" version includes the lines "my mammy's apple poi" and "beneath the ukulele tree."

Alice Faye and Betty Grable in *Tin Pan Alley.*
Twentieth Century-Fox, 1940.

# CHORD CAST

**Tune Ukulele**
**G C E A**

## MAJOR CHORDS

A  A#/B♭  B  C  C#/D♭  D  D#/E♭  E  F  F#/G♭  G  G#/A♭

## MINOR CHORDS

Am  A#m/B♭m  Bm  Cm  C#m/D♭m  Dm  D#m/E♭m  Em  Fm  F#m/G♭m  Gm  G#m/A♭m

## DOMINANT SEVENTH CHORDS

A⁷  A#⁷/B♭⁷  B⁷  C⁷  C#⁷/D♭⁷  D⁷  D#⁷/E♭⁷  E⁷  F⁷  F#⁷/G♭⁷  G⁷  G#⁷/A♭⁷

## DOMINANT NINTH CHORDS

A⁹  A#⁹/B♭⁹  B⁹  C⁹  C#⁹/D♭⁹  D⁹  D#⁹/E♭⁹  E⁹  F⁹  F#⁹/G♭⁹  G⁹  G#⁹/A♭⁹

## MINOR SEVENTH CHORDS

Am⁷  A#m⁷/B♭m⁷  Bm⁷  Cm⁷  C#m⁷/D♭m⁷  Dm⁷  D#m⁷/E♭m⁷  Em⁷  Fm⁷  F#m⁷/G♭m⁷  Gm⁷  G#m⁷/A♭m⁷

## MAJOR SIXTH CHORDS

A⁶  A#⁶/B♭⁶  B⁶  C⁶  C#⁶/D♭⁶  D⁶  D#⁶/E♭⁶  E⁶  F⁶  F#⁶/G♭⁶  G⁶  G#⁶/A♭⁶

8

# MINOR SIXTH CHORDS

Am⁶  A♯m⁶/B♭m⁶  Bm⁶  Cm⁶  C♯m⁶/D♭m⁶  Dm⁶  D♯m⁶/E♭m⁶  Em⁶  Fm⁶  F♯m⁶/G♭m⁶  Gm⁶  G♯m⁶/A♭m⁶

# MAJOR SEVENTH CHORDS

Amaj⁷  A♯maj⁷/B♭maj⁷  Bmaj⁷  Cmaj⁷  C♯maj⁷/D♭maj⁷  Dmaj⁷  D♯maj⁷/E♭maj⁷  Emaj⁷  Fmaj⁷  F♯maj⁷/G♭maj⁷  Gmaj⁷  G♯maj⁷/A♭maj⁷

# DOMINANT SEVENTH CHORDS WITH RAISED FIFTH (7th+5)

A⁷⁺⁵  A♯⁷⁺⁵/B♭⁷⁺⁵  B⁷⁺⁵  C⁷⁺⁵  C♯⁷⁺⁵/D♭⁷⁺⁵  D⁷⁺⁵  D♯⁷⁺⁵/E♭⁷⁺⁵  E⁷⁺⁵  F⁷⁺⁵  F♯⁷⁺⁵/G♭⁷⁺⁵  G⁷⁺⁵  G♯⁷⁺⁵/A♭⁷⁺⁵

# DOMINANT SEVENTH CHORDS WITH LOWERED FIFTH (7th-5)

A⁷⁻⁵  A♯⁷⁻⁵/B♭⁷⁻⁵  B⁷⁻⁵  C⁷⁻⁵  C♯⁷⁻⁵/D♭⁷⁻⁵  D⁷⁻⁵  D♯⁷⁻⁵/E♭⁷⁻⁵  E⁷⁻⁵  F⁷⁻⁵  F♯⁷⁻⁵/G♭⁷⁻⁵  G⁷⁻⁵  G♯⁷⁻⁵/A♭⁷⁻⁵

# AUGMENTED FIFTH CHORDS (aug or +)

Aaug  A♯aug/B♭aug  Baug  Caug  C♯aug/D♭aug  Daug  D♯aug/E♭aug  Eaug  Faug  F♯aug/G♭aug  Gaug  G♯aug/A♭aug

# DIMINISHED SEVENTH CHORDS (dim)

Adim  A♯dim/B♭dim  Bdim  Cdim  C♯dim/D♭dim  Ddim  D♯dim/E♭dim  Edim  Fdim  F♯dim/G♭dim  Gdim  G♯dim/A♭dim

9

# Around The World

## Around The World In 80 Days

Words by
**HAROLD ADAMSON**

Music by
**VICTOR YOUNG**

**FIRST NOTE**

Slow Waltz tempo

A - round the world I've searched for you, I trav - eled on, when hope was gone, to keep a ren - dez - vous. I knew some - where, some - time, some - how, you'd look at me, and I would see the smile you're smil - ing

© 1956 VICTOR YOUNG PUBLICATIONS, INC.
© Renewed 1984 and Assigned to CEBCO MUSIC and LIZA MUSIC CORP. in the United States.
All Rights outside the United States administered by CHAPPELL & CO.
All Rights Reserved   Used by Permission

10

now. It might have been in Coun - ty

G#dim

Down, or in New York, in gay Pa - ree, or e - ven

Am                                    C6

Lon - don Town.     No     more     will

C#dim              G                  E7

I     go   all   a - round     the     world,   for   I   have

Am7            D7             G

found   my   world   in   you. _____

Bing Crosby, Dorothy Lamour and Bob Hope in
*Road To Zanzibar*. Paramount Pictures, 1940.

# As Time Goes By

*Casablanca*

Words and Music by
HERMAN HUPFELD

© 1931 WARNER BROS. INC. (Renewed)
All Rights Reserved   Used by Permission

Moon-light and love \_\_\_\_ songs nev - er out of date,

hearts full of pas - sion, jeal - ous - y and hate;

wom - an needs man \_\_\_\_ and man must have his mate, that

no one can de - ny. It's still the same old sto - ry, a

fight for love and glo - ry, a case of do or die! The

world will al - ways wel - come lov - ers, as time goes by. _____

# Easter Parade

*Easter Parade*

Words and Music by
IRVING BERLIN

(Boy:) In your / (Girl:) In my Eas - ter bon - net, with all the frills up -

on it, you'll / I'll be the grand - est la - dy in the East - er Pa -

rade. I'll / You'll be all in clov - er and when they look you / me

o - ver I'll / you'll be the proud - est fel - low in the

East - er Pa - rade. On the Av - e - nue, Fifth

© Copyright 1933 by Irving Berlin. Copyright Renewed
This Arrangement © Copyright 2003 by the Estate of Irving Berlin
International Copyright Secured All Rights Reserved

**B♭6 / Dm7**

Av - e - nue, the pho - to - graph - ers will

**G7 / C / B♭ / Am / C7 / C7♯5**

snap us, and you'll find that you're in the ro - to - gra - vure. Oh,

**F / C7 / F / F7♯5 / B♭ / G♯dim**

{I could / you may} write a son - net a - bout {your / my} East - er bon - net, and

**F / C7 / F / Dm7 / G7 / C7 / F**

of the girl {I'm / you're} tak - ing to the East - er Pa - rade.

Eddie Cantor in *The Kid From Spain*. Samuel Goldwyn, 1932.

*Collection of Geoffrey R. Rezek*

# For Me And My Gal

*For Me And My Gal*

**Words by**
EDGAR LESLIE and E. RAY GOETZ

**Music by**
GEORGE W. MEYER

**FIRST NOTE**

Moderately, flowing

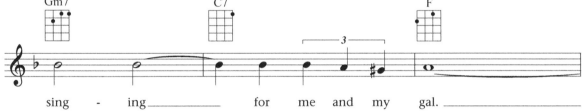

The bells are ring - ing _____

_____ for me and my gal. _____ The birds are

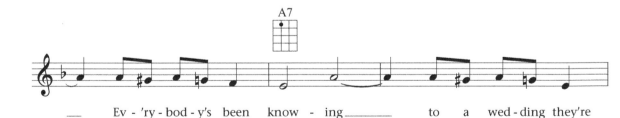

sing - ing _____ for me and my gal. _____

Ev - 'ry - bod - y's been know - ing _____ to a wed - ding they're

go - ing _____ and for weeks they've been sew - ing. _____

© 1917 (Renewed 1945) EMI MILLS MUSIC, INC.
This Arrangement © 2003 by FLEA MARKET MUSIC, INC. (USA) and EMI MILLS MUSIC, INC. (elsewhere)
Print Rights on behalf of EMI MILLS MUSIC, INC. Administered by WARNER BROS. PUBLICATIONS U.S. INC.
All Rights Reserved   Used by Permission

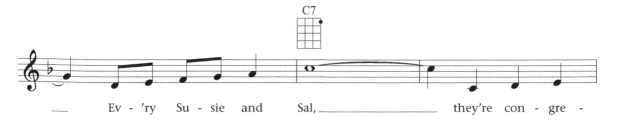

Ev - 'ry Su - sie and Sal,_____ they're con - gre -

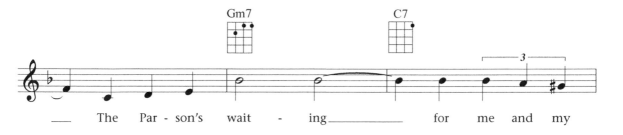

gat - ing_____ for me and my gal. _____

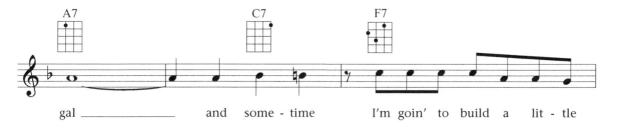

_____ The Par - son's wait - ing_____ for me and my

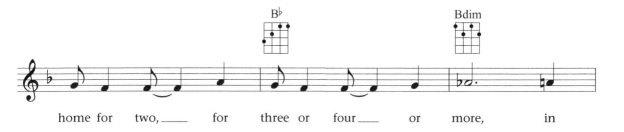

gal _____ and some - time I'm goin' to build a lit - tle

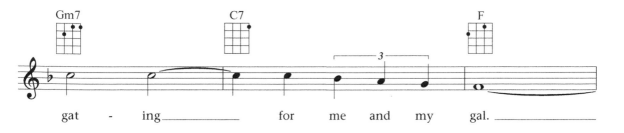

home for two,_____ for three or four___ or more, in

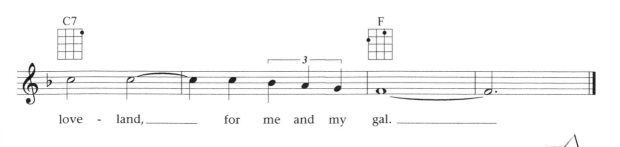

love - land,_____ for me and my gal. _____

# High Hopes

## A Hole In The Head

Words by
**SAMMY CAHN**

Music by
**JIMMY van HEUSEN**

**FIRST NOTE**

Moderately (with a beat)

1. Next time you're found____ with your chin on the ground,__ there's a
2. When trou-bles call____ and your back's to the wall,____ there's a

lot to be learned, __ so look a - round._____
lot to be learned, __ that wall could fall._____

**Refrain**

Just what makes that lit-tle ol' ant____ think he'll move that
Once there was a sil-ly ol' ram,___ thought he'd punch a

rub - ber tree plant;____ an - y - one knows____ an
hole in a dam;____ no one could make____ that

© 1959 by SINCAP PRODUCTIONS, INC.
© 1959 by MARAVILLE MUSIC CORP.
Copyright Renewed by MARAVILLE MUSIC CORP.
All Rights Reserved    Used by Permission

ant can't____ move a rub-ber tree plant. But he's got
ram scram,____ he kept but-tin' that dam. 'Cause he had
3. So keep your

high_____ hopes, he's got high_____
high_____ hopes, he had high_____
high_____ hopes, keep your high_____

hopes, he's got high ap - ple pie in the
hopes, he had high ap - ple pie in the
hopes, keep those high ap - ple pie in the

sky_____ hopes. So an - y time you're get - tin' low,
sky_____ hopes. So an - y time you're feel - in' bad,
sky_____ hopes. A prob - lem's just a toy____ bal - loon,

'stead of let - tin' go, just re - mem - ber that
'stead of feel - in' sad, just re - mem - ber that
they'll be burst - ing soon, they're just bound____ to go

19

ant.
ram.
"pop!"

Oops! There goes an -
Oops! There goes a
Oops! There goes an -

oth - er rub - ber tree plant. *(Oops! There goes an -*
bil - lion kil - o - watt dam. *(Oops! There goes a*
oth - er prob - lem, ker - plop! *(Oops! There goes an -*

*oth - er rub - ber tree plant)* Oops! There goes an -
*bil - lion kil - o - watt dam)* Oops! There goes a
*oth - er prob - lem, ker - plop!)* Oops! There goes an -

**To Coda** ⊕                               **2nd time, D.S. al Coda**

oth - er rub - ber tree plant!
bill - ion kil - o - watt dam!
oth - er prob - lem, ker -

⊕ **Coda**

plop!                Ker - plop!

20

# Honolulu

*Honolulu*

**Words by**
**GUS KAHN**

**Music by**
**HARRY WARREN**

I'm on my mer-ry way, ____
I'm on a hol-i-day, ____ I mean I'm on my
way to Hon - o - lu - lu. ____
The days just drift a - long, ____ the nights are
filled with song, ____ I hope that I'm not wrong on Hon - o -

© 1939 (Renewed 1966) EMI FEIST CATALOG INC.
Rights for the Extended Term of Copyright in the U.S. Assigned to
KEYES GILBERT MUSIC COMPANY (C/o The Songwriters Guild of America) and WB MUSIC CORP.
Print Rights on behalf of EMI FEIST CATALOG, INC. Administered by WARNER BROS. PUBLICATIONS U.S.
INC. All Rights Reserved    Used by Permission

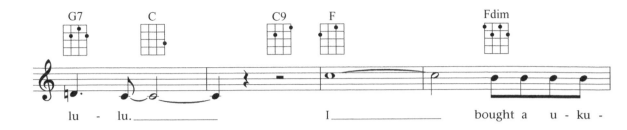

lu - lu._____ I_____ bought a u - ku -

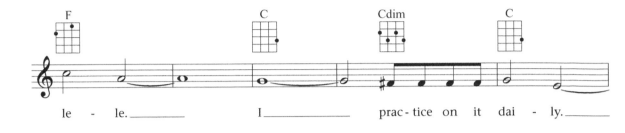

le - le._____ I_____ prac - tice on it dai - ly._____

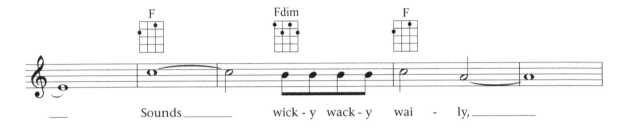

___ Sounds_____ wick - y wack - y wai - ly,_____

my_____ hu - la hu - la song._____ I know it's

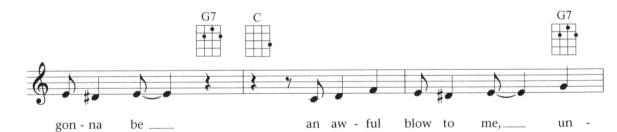

gon - na be ___ an aw - ful blow to me,___ un -

less I find ro - mance in Hon - o - lu - lu,_____

22

I know just how it looks, from the pret - ty pic - ture books, so please don't dis - ap - point me, Hon - o - lu - lu, my Hon - o - lu - lu by the cor - al sea.

Shirley Temple at Waikiki Beach. Hawaii State Archives.

# Hooray For Hollywood

*Hollywood Hotel*

**Words by**
**JOHNNY MERCER**

**Music by**
**RICHARD A. WHITING**

© 1937, 1938 WARNER BROS. INC.  Copyrights Renewed
All Rights Reserved   Used by Permission

maid, if she danc - es with or with - out a fan, ___
tos, with their hair in rib - bons and legs in tights, ___

— hoo - ray for Hol - ly - wood! _____ Where you're ter -
You may be

rif - ic if you're e - ven good, _____ where an - y -
home - ly in your neigh - bor - hood, _____ but if you

one at all from Shir - ley Tem - ple to Ai - mee Sem -
think that you can be an ac - tor, see Mis - ter Fac -

ple is e - qual - ly ___ un - der - stood, ___
tor, he'd make a mon - key look good, ___

— go out and try your luck, ___ you might be
with - in a half an hour, ___ you'll look like

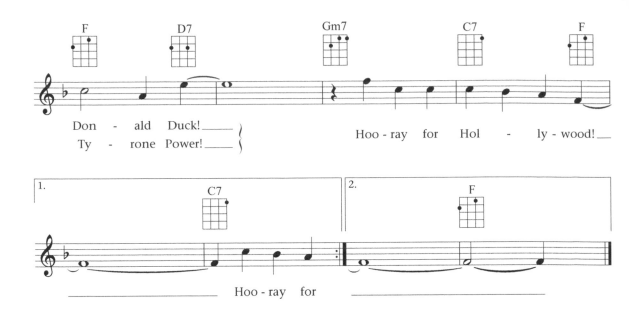

F    D7    Gm7    C7    F

Don - ald Duck!____
Ty - rone Power!____
Hoo - ray for Hol - ly - wood!__

1.    C7

2.    F

_____ Hoo - ray for _____

—Hollywood Boulevard at Night, Hollywood, California

# My Favorite Things

## The Sound Of Music

Words by
**OSCAR HAMMERSTEIN II**

Music by
**RICHARD RODGERS**

Rain - drops on ros - es and whisk - ers on kit - tens,

bright cop - per ket - tles and warm wool - en mit - tens,

brown pa - per pack - ag - es tied up with strings,

these are a few of my fa - vor - ite things.

Cream - col - ored pon - ies and crisp ap - ple

Copyright © 1959 by Richard Rodgers and Oscar Hammerstein II  Copyright Renewed
This Arrangement © Copyright 2003 by Williamson Music.
Williamson Music owner of publication and allied rights throughout the world.
International Copyright Secured All Rights Reserved

27

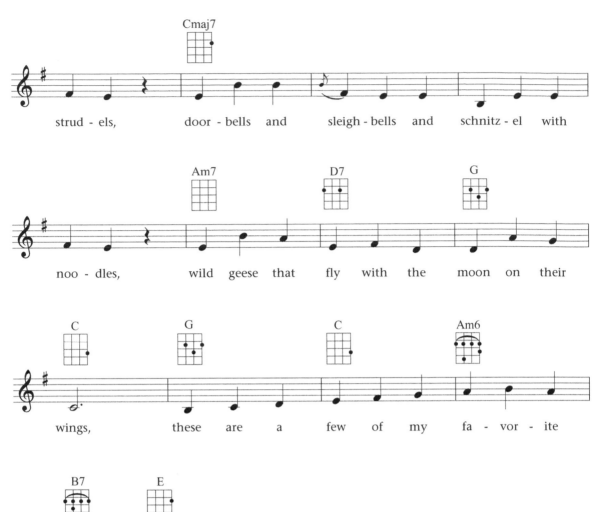

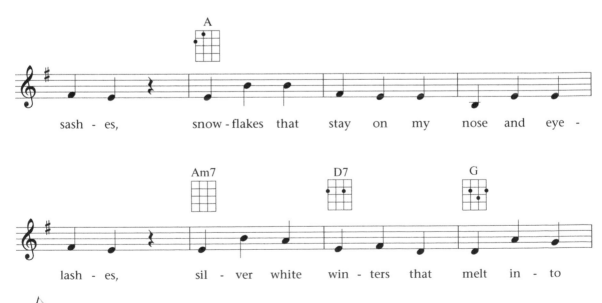

springs,     these   are   a   few   of   my   fa - vor - ite

things.     When   the   dog   bites,     when   the   bee   stings,

when   I'm   feel - ing   sad, _____     I

sim - ply   re - mem - ber   my   fa - vor - ite   things   and

then   I   don't   feel     so

bad. _____

29

# I Can't Give You Anything But Love

*Bringing Up Baby*

Words by
**DOROTHY FIELDS**

Music by
**JIMMY McHUGH**

FIRST NOTE

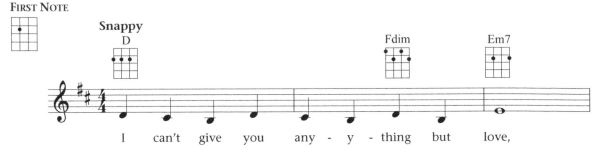

I can't give you any - y - thing but love,

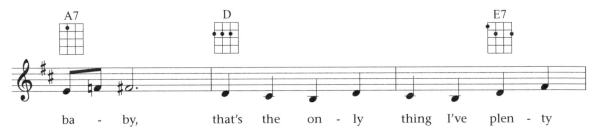

ba - by, that's the on - ly thing I've plen - ty

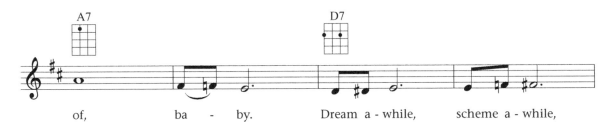

of, ba - by. Dream a - while, scheme a - while,

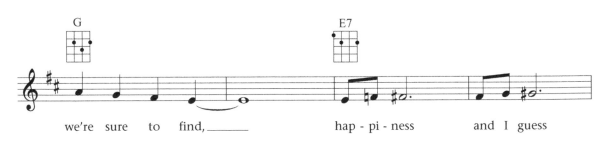

we're sure to find, _____ hap - pi - ness and I guess

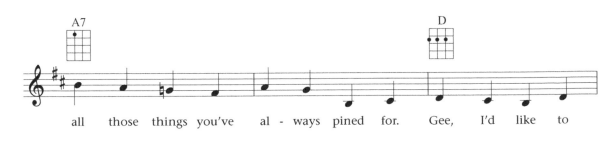

all those things you've al - ways pined for. Gee, I'd like to

© 1928 (Renewed 1956) COTTON CLUB PUBLISHING and ALDI MUSIC.
This arrangement © 2003 COTTON CLUB PUBLISHING and ALDI MUSIC.
Rights for COTTON CLUB MUSIC Controlled and Administered by EMI APRIL MUSIC, INC.
Rights for ALDI MUSIC administered by The Songwriters Guild of America
All Rights Reserved International Copyright Secured Used by Permission

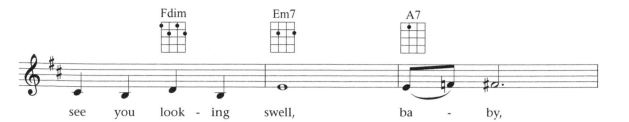

see    you    look - ing    swell,              ba  -  by,

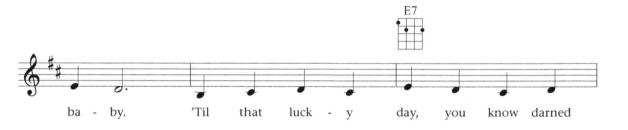

dia - mond    brace - lets    Wool - worth    does - n't    sell,

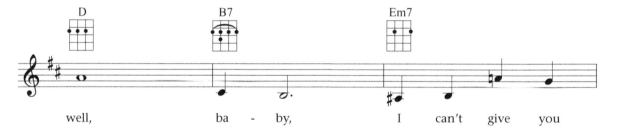

ba  -  by.        'Til    that    luck - y    day,    you    know    darned

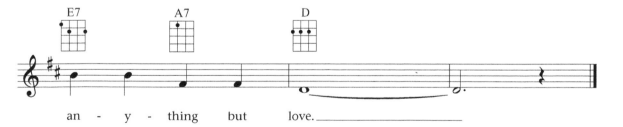

well,                ba  -  by,            I    can't    give    you

an  -  y - thing    but    love. _____

# It's Only A Paper Moon

*Take A Chance*
*Too Young To Know*
*Paper Moon*

Words by
**BILLY ROSE and E. Y. HARBURG**

Music by
**HAROLD ARLEN**

© 1933 (Renewed) CHAPPELL & CO., GLOCCA MORRA MUSIC and S.A. MUSIC CO. WARNER BROS. INC. (Renewed)
Rights for the Extended Renewal Term in the U.S. Assigned to GLOCCA MORRA MUSIC, CHAPPELL & CO. & SA MUSIC.
This arrangement © 2003 CHAPPELL & CO., GLOCCA MORRA MUSIC and S.A. MUSIC CO.
All Rights Reserved  Used by Permission

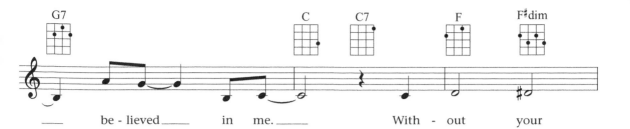

_\_ be - lieved \_\_\_ in me. \_\_\_ With - out your_

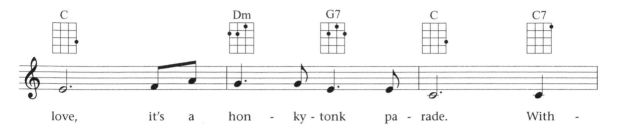

_love, it's a hon - ky - tonk pa - rade. With -_

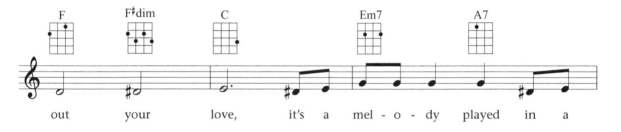

_out your love, it's a mel - o - dy played in a_

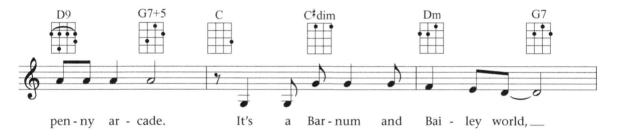

_pen - ny ar - cade. It's a Bar - num and Bai - ley world, \_\_\__

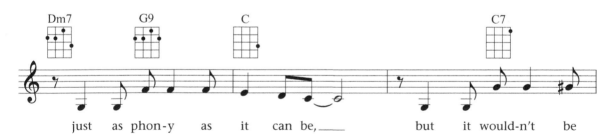

_just as phon - y as it can be, \_\_\_ but it would-n't be_

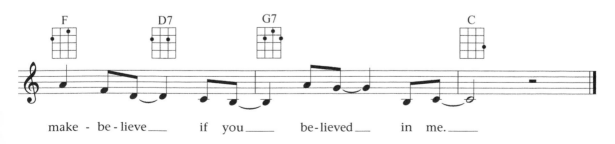

_make - be - lieve \_\_\_ if you \_\_\_ be - lieved \_\_\_ in me. \_\_\__

# A Kiss To Build A Dream On

## The Strip

Words and Music by
BERT KALMAR, HARRY RUBY,
and OSCAR HAMMERSTEIN II

FIRST NOTE

Slowly

1. Give me a kiss to build a
2. Give me a kiss be - fore you
3. Give me your lips for just a

dream on and my im - ag - i -
leave me and my im - ag - i -
mo - ment, and my im - ag - i -

na - tion will thrive up - on that kiss.
na - tion will feed my hun - gry heart.
na - tion will make that mo - ment live.

*To Coda*

Sweet - heart, I ask no more than this, a kiss to build a
Leave me one thing be - fore we part, a kiss to build a
Give me what you a - lone can give, a kiss to build a

© 1935 (Renewed 1963) METRO-GOLDWYN-MAYER INC.
All Rights Controlled by EMI MILLER CATALOG INC. (Publishing)
and WARNER BROS. PUBLICATIONS U.S. INC. (Print)
All Rights Reserved   Used by Permission

dream on._____ dream on._____ When I'm a

lone _____ with my fan - cies I'll _____ be with

you, weav - ing ro - manc - es mak-ing be - lieve they're

*D.C. al Coda*     ⊕ *Coda*

true.     dream on._____

# Love Is A Many-Splendored Thing

*Love Is A Many-Splendored Thing*

**Words by**
PAUL FRANCIS WEBSTER

**Music by**
SAMMY FAIN

FIRST NOTE

© 1955 TWENTIETH CENTURY MUSIC CORPORATION © Renewed 1983 EMI MILLER CATALOG INC.
All Rights Controlled by EMI MILLER CATALOG INC. (Publishing)
and WARNER BROS. PUBLICATIONS U.S. INC. (Print)
All Rights Reserved    Used by Permission

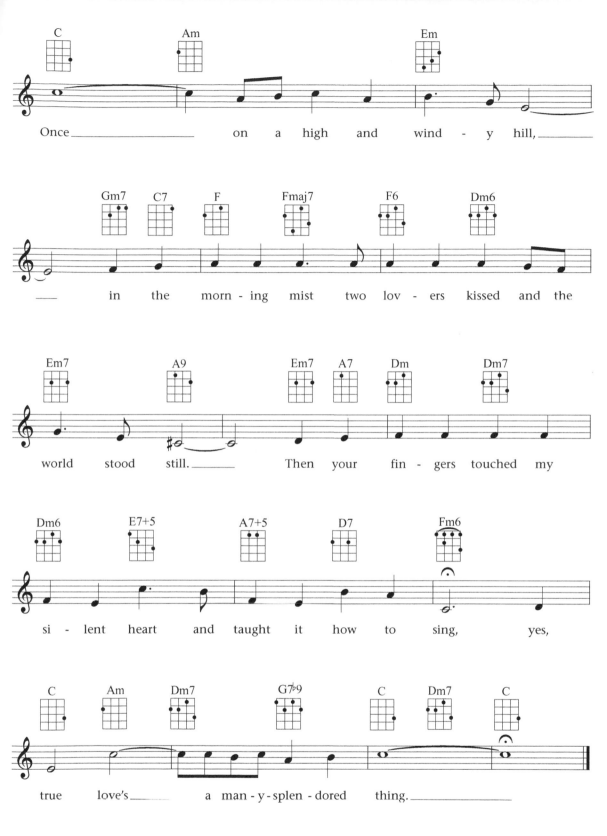

Once _____ on a high and wind - y hill, _____

_____ in the morn - ing mist two lov - ers kissed and the

world stood still. _____ Then your fin - gers touched my

si - lent heart and taught it how to sing, yes,

true love's _____ a man - y - splen - dored thing. _____

# Love Is Here To Stay

## The Goldwyn Follies
## An American In Paris

Words by
**IRA GERSHWIN**

Music by
**GEORGE GERSHWIN**

FIRST NOTE

Flowing

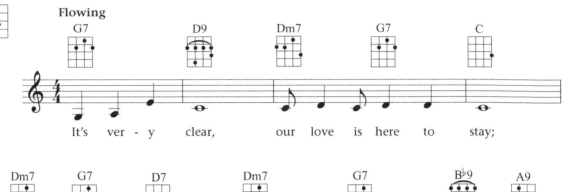

It's ver - y clear, our love is here to stay;

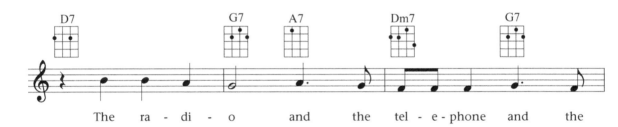

not for a year but ev - er and a day.

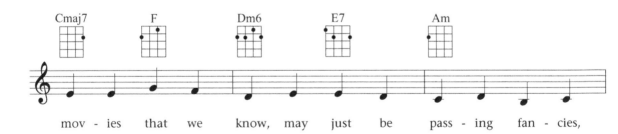

The ra - di - o and the tel - e - phone and the

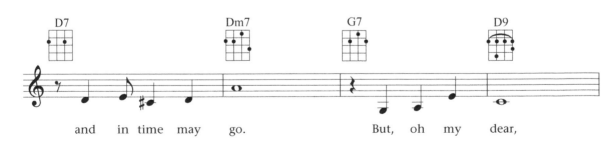

mov - ies that we know, may just be pass - ing fan - cies,

and in time may go. But, oh my dear,

© 1938 (Renewed 1965) GEORGE GERSHWIN MUSIC and IRA GERSHWIN MUSIC
All Rights Administered by WB MUSIC CORP.
All Rights Reserved   Used by Permission

**Dm7 · G7 · C · Dm7 G7 · D7**

our  love  is  here  to  stay;  to - geth - er  we're

**Dm7 · G7 · B♭9 A9 D7 · G7 · A7**

go - ing  a long, long  way.  In time, the Rock - ies may crum - ble, Gib-

**Dm7 · G7 · B♭9 · A7 · Dm7 Adim**

ral - tar may tum - ble,  they're on - ly made  of  clay,  but

**C · Dm7 G7 · C**

our  love  is  here  to  stay._____

Leslie Caron and Gene Kelly in
*An American In Paris.* MGM, 1951.

39

Collection of Miss Ewa Noskowicz

Will Rogers relaxes on the movie set of
*Doubling For Romeo*. Goldwyn Pictures, 1921.

Mia Farrow and Jeff Daniels
in *The Purple Rose of Cairo*.
Orion, 1985.

Bob Hope and Martha
Raye in *College Swing*.
Paramount Pictures, 1938.

Barry Gordon, Jason Robards and Barbara Harris in
*A Thousand Clowns*. United Artists, 1966.

The Caine Mutiny. Columbia Pictures, 1954.

Martha Raye in *Waikiki Wedding*.
Paramount Pictures, 1937.

Collection of Geoffrey R. Rezek

Eddie Bracken, Betty Hutton, Rudy Vallee, Mary Martin
and Dick Powell in *Happy Go Lucky*.
Paramount Pictures, 1942.

Collection of Miss Ewa Noskowicz

Lawrence Gray and Marion Davies in
*Marianne*. MGM, 1929.

# Makin' Whoopee!

## Whoopee

Words by
GUS KAHN

Music by
WALTER DONALDSON

© 1928 (Renewed) WB MUSIC CORP.
Rights for the Extended Term in the U.S. Assigned to GILBERT KEYES MUSIC
and DONALDSON PUBLISHING CORP. All Rights Reserved   Used By Permission

whoop-ee! ... Pic-ture a lit-tle love-nest,
whoop-ee! ... He does-n't make much mon-ey,

down where the ros-es cling. ... Pic-ture the same sweet
on-ly five thou-sand per. ... Some judge who thinks he's

love-nest, think what a year can bring.____ He's wash-ing
fun-ny, say's "You'll pay six to her." ____ He says, "Now

dish-es____ and ba-by clothes,____ he's so am-
Judge,____ sup-pose I fail?"____ The judge says,

bi-tious __ he e-ven sews,____ but don't for-get, folks,__ that's what you
"Budge____ right in-to jail.____You'd bet-ter keep her,____ I think it's

*D.C. (Take Repeats)*

get, folks,____ for mak-in' whoop-ee!_____
cheap-er____ than mak-in' whoop-ee!"_____

43

# Moon River

*Breakfast At Tiffany's*

Lyric by
**JOHNNY MERCER**

Music by
**HENRY MANCINI**

FIRST NOTE

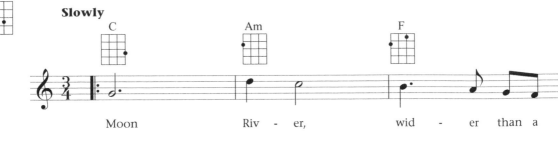

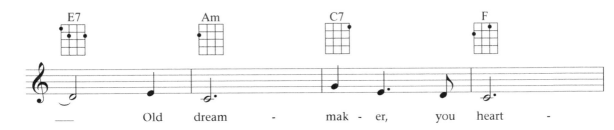

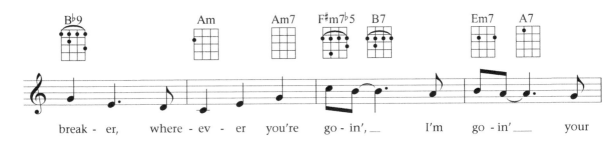

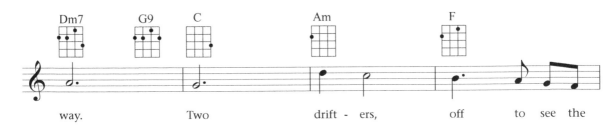

Copyright © 1961 (Renewed 1989) by Famous Music Corporation
This Arrangement © Copyright 2003 by Famous Music Corporation
International Copyright Secured  All Rights Reserved

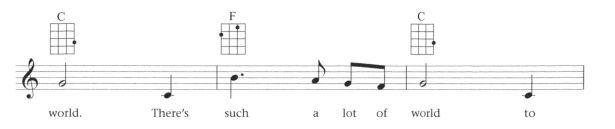

world. There's such a lot of world to

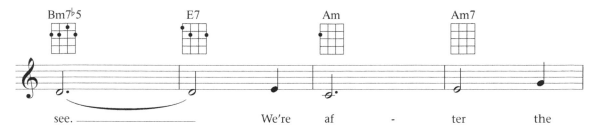

see. _____ We're af - ter the

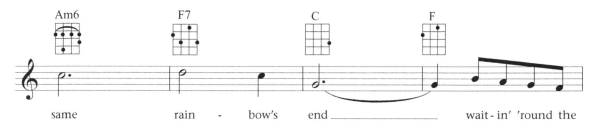

same rain - bow's end _____ wait - in' 'round the

bend, _____ my huck - le - ber - ry friend, Moon

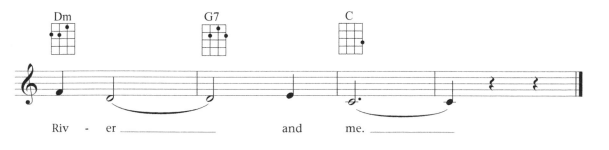

Riv - er _____ and me. _____

# My Own True Love

*Gone With The Wind*

**Words by**
**MACK DAVID**

**Music by**
**MAX STEINER**

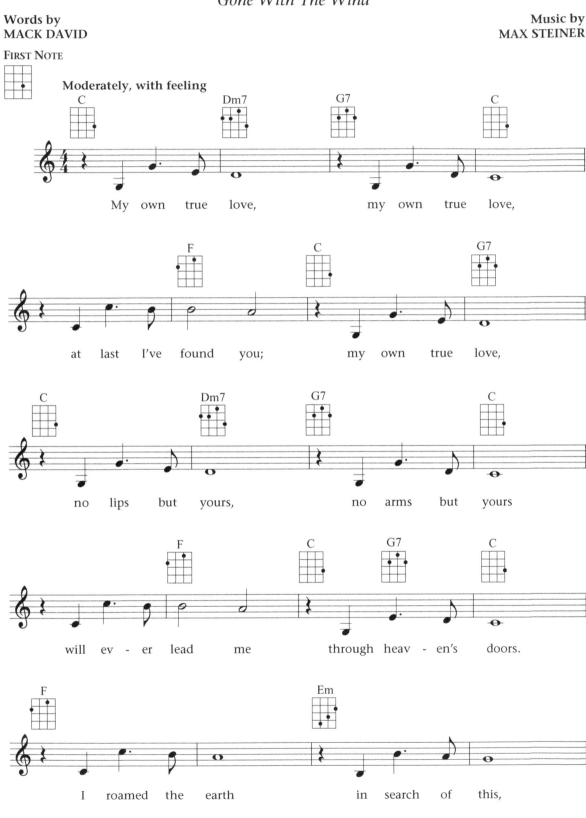

© 1940, 1954 WARNER BROS. INC.  Copyrights Renewed
All Rights Reserved    Used by Permission

I knew I'd know you, know you by your kiss,

and by your kiss you've shown true love,

I'm yours for - ev - er, my own true love.

# On The Good Ship Lollipop

*Bright Eyes*

Words and Music by SIDNEY CLARE
and RICHARD A. WHITING

FIRST NOTE

Jauntily

On the good ship ___ Lol-li-pop, ___ it's a sweet trip ___ to a

can-dy shop ___ where bon-bons play _____ on the sun-ny beach of

pep-per-mint bay. _____ Lem-on-ade stands ___

ev-'ry-where, ___ Crack-er Jack bands ___ fill the air ___ and

there you are _____ hap-py land-ing on a choc-o-late bar.

© 1934 (Renewed 1962) by Bourne Co. and Whiting Publishing and MOVIETONE MUSIC CORPORATION
Copyright Renewed
All Rights for MOVIETONE MUSIC CORPORATION Assigned to WB MUSIC CORP.
All Rights for the Extended Renewal Term in the U.S. Administered by SHIP LOLLIPOP PUBLISHING
c/o THE SONG-WRITERS GUILD OF AMERICA and BOURNE CO.
This Arrangement © Copyright 2003 by Bourne Co. and Whiting Publishing
All Rights Reserved  International Copyright Secured  Used by Permission

See the sug-ar bowl___ do a Toot-sie Roll ___ with the big bad dev-il's food cake.___ If you eat too much___ ooh! ooh!___ You'll a-wake with a "tum-my" ache.___ On the good ship ___ Lol-li-pop, ___ it's a night trip___ in-to bed you hop___ { with this com-mand:___ "All a-board for / and dream a-way___ on the good ship

1. can-dy land."

2. On the Lol-li-pop!___

# Over The Rainbow

## The Wizard Of Oz

Words by
**E. Y. HARBURG**

Music by
**HAROLD ARLEN**

FIRST NOTE

Moderately

Some - where    o - ver  the  rain - bow    way    up

high,          there's    a        land  that  I  heard  of

once  in  a  lul - la - by.            Some - where

o - ver  the  rain - bow    skies    are    blue,

and       the       dreams  that  you  dare  to    dream real - ly  do  come

© 1938 (Renewed 1966) METRO-GOLDWYN-MAYER INC. ©1939 (Renewed 1967) EMI FEIST CATALOG INC.
Rights throughout the World Controlled by EMI FEIST CATALOG INC. (Publishing)
and WARNER BROS. PUBLICATIONS U.S. INC. (Print)
All Rights Reserved    Used by Permission

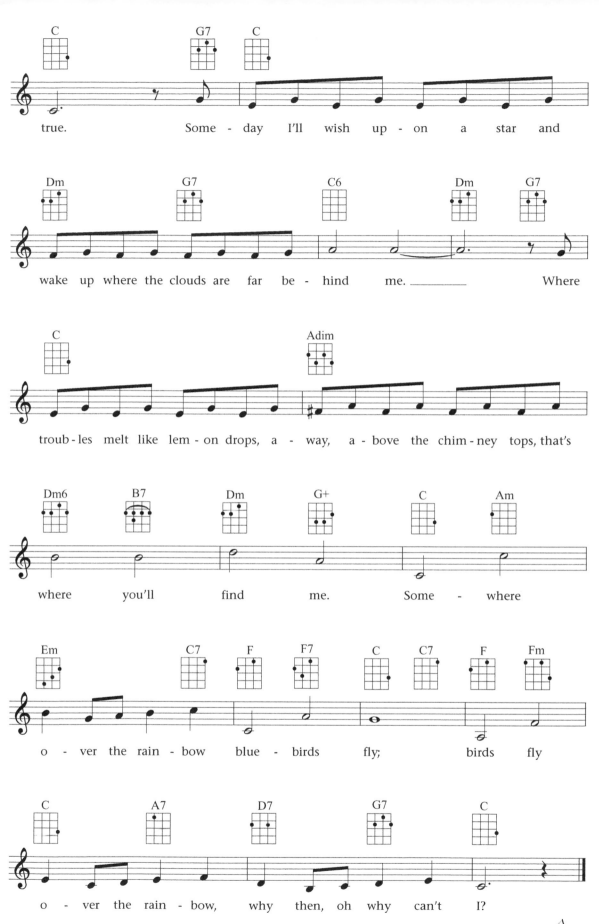

true. Some - day I'll wish up - on a star and

wake up where the clouds are far be - hind me. _____ Where

troub - les melt like lem - on drops, a - way, a - bove the chim - ney tops, that's

where you'll find me. Some - where

o - ver the rain - bow blue - birds fly; birds fly

o - ver the rain - bow, why then, oh why can't I?

51

# Pennies From Heaven

*Pennies From Heaven*

Words by
JOHN BURKE

Music by
ARTHUR JOHNSTON

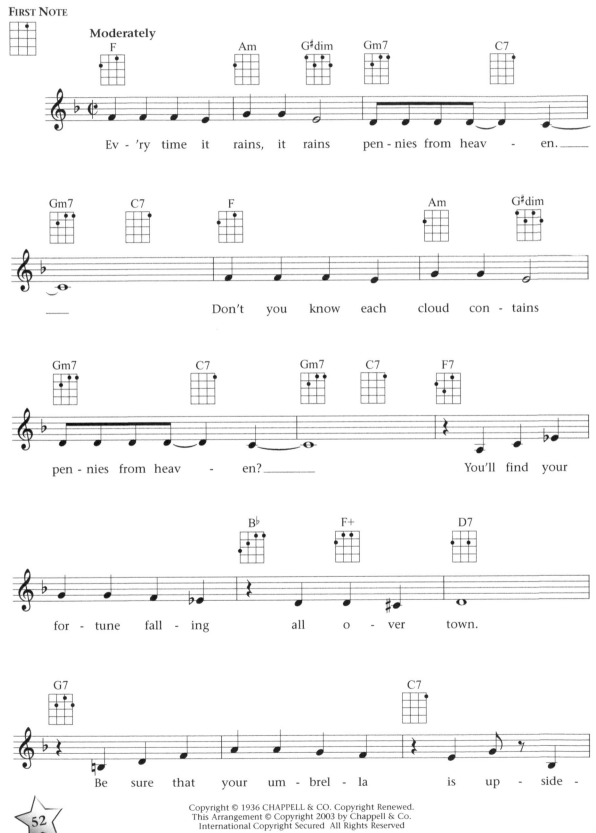

Ev - 'ry time it rains, it rains pen - nies from heav - en.

Don't you know each cloud con - tains pen - nies from heav - en?

You'll find your for - tune fall - ing all o - ver town.

Be sure that your um - brel - la is up - side -

Copyright © 1936 CHAPPELL & CO. Copyright Renewed.
This Arrangement © Copyright 2003 by Chappell & Co.
International Copyright Secured  All Rights Reserved

down.  Trade them for a pack - age of

sun - shine and flow - ers. _____ If you want the

things you love, you must have show - ers. _____

So when you hear it thun - der, don't run un - der a tree, ___

___ there'll be pen - nies from heav - en for

you and me. _____

53

# Runnin' Wild

*Some Like It Hot*

**Words by**
**JOE GREY and LEO WOOD**

**Music by**
**A. HARRINGTON GIBBS**

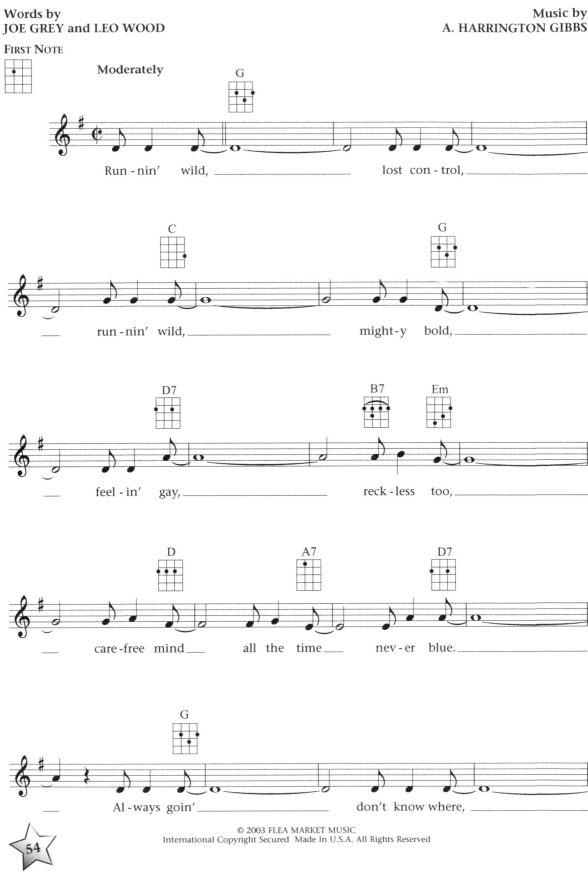

© 2003 FLEA MARKET MUSIC
International Copyright Secured  Made In U.S.A. All Rights Reserved

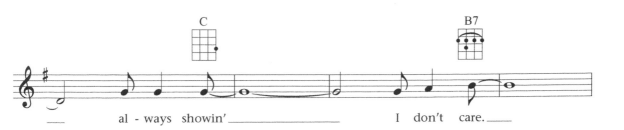

al - ways showin' _____ I don't care. ___

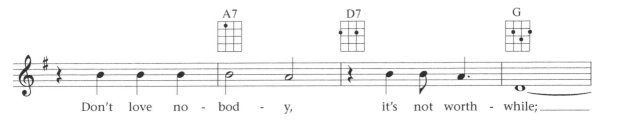

Don't love no - bod - y, it's not worth - while; _____

___ all a - lone, ___ run - nin' wild. _____

Marilyn Monroe shimmies with her uke in *Some Like It Hot*. United Artists, 1959.

*Collection of Geoffrey R. Rezek*

# The Shadow Of Your Smile

*The Sandpiper*

**Words by**
PAUL FRANCIS WEBSTER

**Music by**
JOHNNY MANDEL

© 1965 METRO-GOLDWYN-MAYER INC.
© Renewed 1993 EMI MILLER CATALOG INC.
All Rights Controlled by EMI MILLER CATALOG INC. (Publishing)
and WARNER BROS. PUBLICATIONS U.S. INC. (Print)
All Rights Reserved   Used by Permission

Dm     G9     Gm7

high,_____ a tear-drop kissed your lips and

C9     Am7♭5     D7♭9     Gm7

so did I._____ Now when I re-mem-ber spring____

B♭m7   E♭13     Am7    E♭9♭5   Am7   D7♭9

___ all the joy that love can bring,_____ I will be re -

G13    D♭9♭5   Gm7     C7♭9     F    F6/9

mem - ber-ing_____ the shad-ow of your smile._____

Lovely starlet Dorothy Abbott in *Road To Rio*. Paramount Pictures, 1948.

# Singin' In The Rain

*The Hollywood Revue Of 1929*
*Singin' In The Rain*

**Words by**
**ARTHUR FREED**

**Music by**
**NACIO HERB BROWN**

© 1929 (Renewed 1957) METRO-GOLDWYN-MAYER INC.
All Rights Controlled by EMI ROBBINS CATALOG INC. (Publishing)
and WARNER BROS. PUBLICATIONS U.S. INC. (Print)
All Rights Reserved

place. Come on with the rain, I've a smile on my

face, I'll walk down the lane with a hap - py re -

frain, and sing-in', just sing-in' in the rain.

Jack Benny and Cliff Edwards in
*The Hollywood Revue of 1929*. MGM.

# Smile

## Modern Times

Words by
**JOHN TURNER and GEOFFREY PARSONS**

Music by
**CHARLES CHAPLIN**

Smile, tho' your heart is ach - ing, smile, e - ven tho' it's break - ing, when there are clouds in the sky, you'll get by, if you smile through your fear and sor - row, smile and may - be to - mor - row, you'll see the sun come shin - ing through for you. Light up your face with glad - ness, hide ev - 'ry

© Copyright 1954 by Bourne Co. Copyright Renewed
This Arrangement © Copyright 2003 by Bourne Co.
All Rights Reserved   International Copyright Secured

C      Cdim      Dm7

trace of sad - ness, al - tho' a tear may be ev - er so

A7♭9      Dm7      Fm

near, that's the time you must keep on try - ing, smile what's the

B♭9      Cmaj7      Dm7

use of cry - ing, you'll find that life is still worth - while, if

G7      C      B♭9      C

you'll just smile. _____

# Swinging On A Star

*Going My Way*

**Words by**
JOHNNY BURKE

**Music by**
JIMMY van HEUSEN

FIRST NOTE

Moderately bright

| D7 | G7 | Gm7 | C7 |

1. Would you like to swing on a star, car-ry moon-beams home in a

| F | D7 | G7 | Gm7 | C7 |

jar, _____ and be bet-ter off than you are, or would you rath-er be a

| F | F | B♭ | F | B♭ |

mule? _____ A mule is an an-i-mal with long fun-ny ears, he

2. pig is an an-i-mal with dirt on his face, his

3. fish won't do an-y-thing but swim in a brook, he

| F | B♭ | F | G7 |

kicks up at an-y-thing he hears. _____ His back is brawn-y and his

shoes are a ter-ri-ble dis-grace. _____ He's got no man-ners when he

can't write his name or read a book. _____ To fool the peo-ple is his

| C | Dm7 | G7 |

brain is weak, _____ he's just plain stu-pid with a

eats his food, _____ he's fat and la-zy and ex-

on-ly thought, _____ and though he's slip-per-y, he

© Copyright 1944 by Burke & Van Heusen Inc., a division of Bourne Co.
and Dorsey Bros. Music, a division of Music Sales Corp.
Copyright Renewed. This Arrangement © Copyright 2003 by Burke & Van Heusen Inc.,
a division of Bourne Co. and Dorsey Bros. Music, a division of Music Sales Corp.
All Rights Reserved   International Copyright Secured

stub - born streak. And, by the way, if you hate to go to school,
treme - ly rude. But if you don't care a feath - er or a fig,
still gets caught. But then if that sort of life is what you wish,

you may grow up to be a mule._____ Or would you like to swing on a
you may grow up to be a pig._____ Or would you like to swing on a
you may grow up to be a fish.._____ And all the mon - keys aren't in the

star, car - ry moon - beams home in a jar,_____ and be
star, car - ry moon - beams home in a jar,_____ and be
zoo, ev - 'ry day you meet quite a few,_____ so you

bet - ter off than you are. Or would you rath - er be a
bet - ter off than you are. Or would you rath - er be a
see it's all up to you. You can be bet - ter than you

**1., 2.** | **3.**

pig?_____ A
fish?_____ A

3. are, you could be swing - ing on a star.

# Thanks For The Memory

## The Big Broadcast Of 1938

Words and Music by
LEO ROBIN and RALPH RAINGER

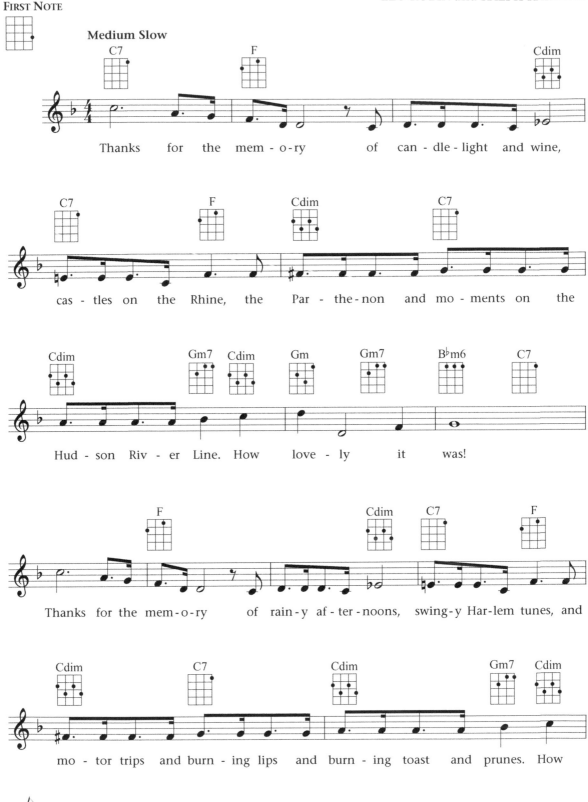

Copyright © 1937 (Renewed 1964) by Paramount Music Corporation
This Arrangement © Copyright 2003 by Paramount Music Corporation
International Copyright Secured   All Rights Reserved

love - ly it was! Ma - ny's the time that we

feast - ed and ma - ny's the time that we fast - ed. Oh,

well, it was swell while it last - ed, we did have fun and

no harm done. And thanks for the mem - o - ry of

sun-burns at the shore, sights in Sing - a - pore. You might have been a head-ache, but you

nev - er were a bore, so thank you so much.____

# True Love

*High Society*

**Words and Music by**
**COLE PORTER**

Copyright © 1955, 1956 by CHAPPELL & CO.
Copyrights Renewed, Assigned to Robert H. Montgomery, Trustee of the COLE PORTER MUSICAL & LITERARY PROPERTY TRUSTS
This Arrangement © Copyright 2003 by Robert H. Montgomery,
Trustee of the COLE PORTER MUSICAL & LITERARY PROPERTY TRUSTS.
CHAPPELL & CO. owner of publication and allied rights throughout the world.
International Copyright Secured   All Rights Reserved

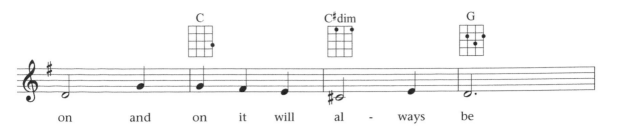

on and on it will al - ways be

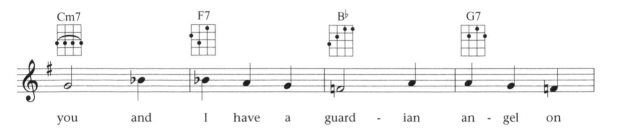

true love, true love. For

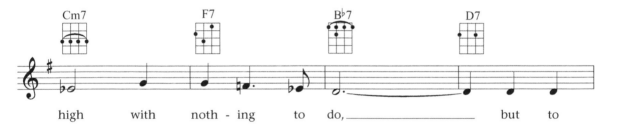

you and I have a guard - ian an - gel on

high with noth - ing to do, _____ but to

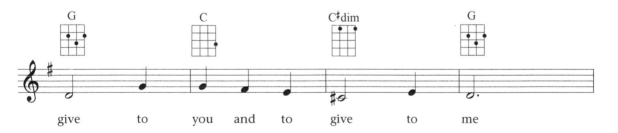

give to you and to give to me

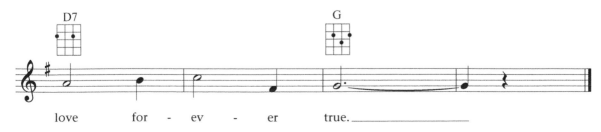

love for - ev - er true. _____

# The Way You Look Tonight

## Swing Time

**Words by**
DOROTHY FIELDS

**Music by**
JEROME KERN

FIRST NOTE

**Slow and lyrically**

C  Am  Dm7

1. Some - day when I'm aw - f'ly
love - ly with your smile so

G7  Em7  A7♭9  Dm7

low, when the world is cold, I will feel a
warm and your world cheek so soft; there is noth - ing

G7  C7  F  Dm7

glow just think - ing of you, and the way you
for me but to of love you, just the way you

G7  C  Am  Dm7  G7  **1.** C  D♯dim

look to - night. _____
look to - night. _____

Dm7  G7  **2.** C  D♯dim  Dm7  G7  E♭maj7

2. Oh, but you're With each

© 1936 (Renewed) Universal - PolyGram International Publishing, Inc. and
ALDI MUSIC CO. (Administered by THE SONGWRITERS GUILD OF AMERICA)
All Rights Reserved    Used by Permission

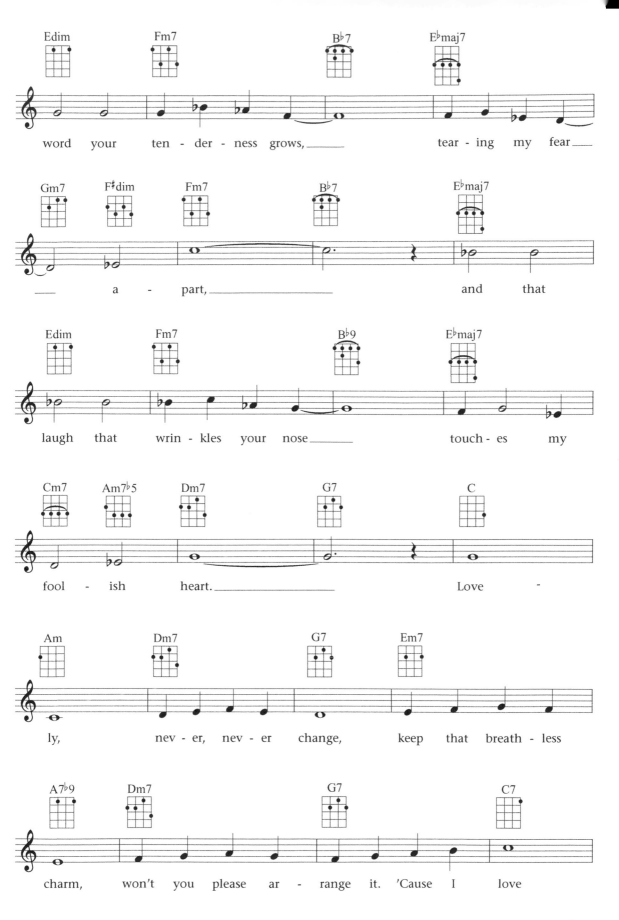

word  your  ten - der - ness  grows, _____  tear - ing  my  fear ____

____  a  -  part, _____  and  that

laugh  that  wrin - kles  your  nose _____  touch - es  my

fool - ish  heart. _____  Love  -

ly,  nev - er,  nev - er  change,  keep  that  breath - less

charm,  won't  you  please  ar - range  it.  'Cause  I  love

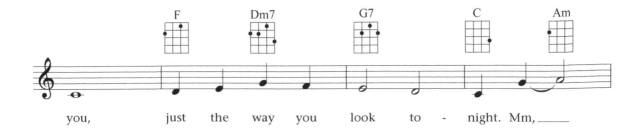

you,        just    the    way    you    look    to  -  night. Mm, _____

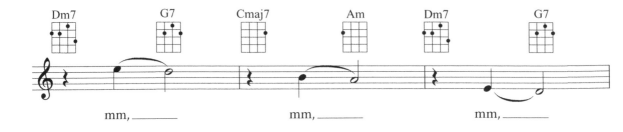

mm, _____        mm, _____        mm, _____

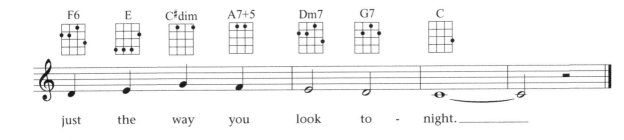

just    the    way    you    look    to  -  night. _____

Ginger Rogers in
*Stage Door.*
RKO, 1937.

# What Are You Doing The Rest Of Your Life?

*The Happy Ending*

**Words by**
ALAN and MARILYN BERGMAN

**Music by**
MICHEL LEGRAND

**FIRST NOTE**

*Moderately, with feeling*

Fm    Fm/E

What are you do - ing the rest of your life? _____

Fm/E♭    Fm/D    D♭maj7

_____ North and south and east and west of your life? _____

B♭m7

_____ I have on - ly one re - quest of your life: _____

Gm7♭5    Gm7/C    C7

_____ that you spend it all with me! _____ All the sea - sons and the

Fm    Fm/E    Fm/E♭    Fm/D

times of your days, _____ all the nick - els and the

© 1969 UNITED ARTISTS MUSIC COMPANY, INC. Copyright Renewed
All Rights Controlled by EMI U CATALOG INC. (Publishing) and WARNER BROS. PUBLICATIONS U.S. INC. (Print)
All Rights Reserved   Used by Permission

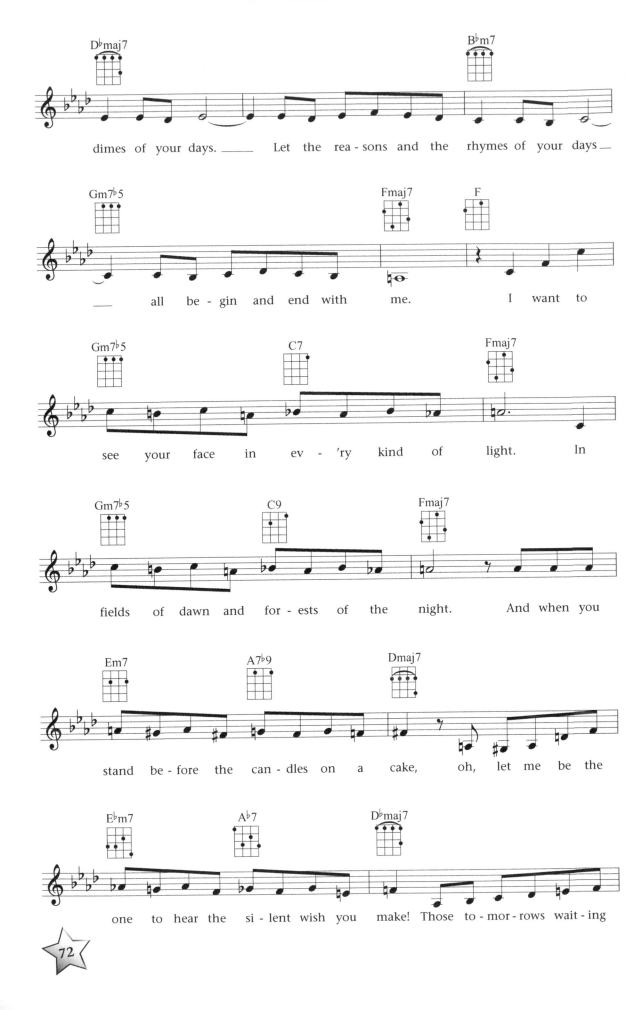

dimes of your days. _____ Let the rea - sons and the rhymes of your days ___

___ all be - gin and end with me. I want to

see your face in ev - 'ry kind of light. In

fields of dawn and for - ests of the night. And when you

stand be - fore the can - dles on a cake, oh, let me be the

one to hear the si - lent wish you make! Those to - mor - rows wait - ing

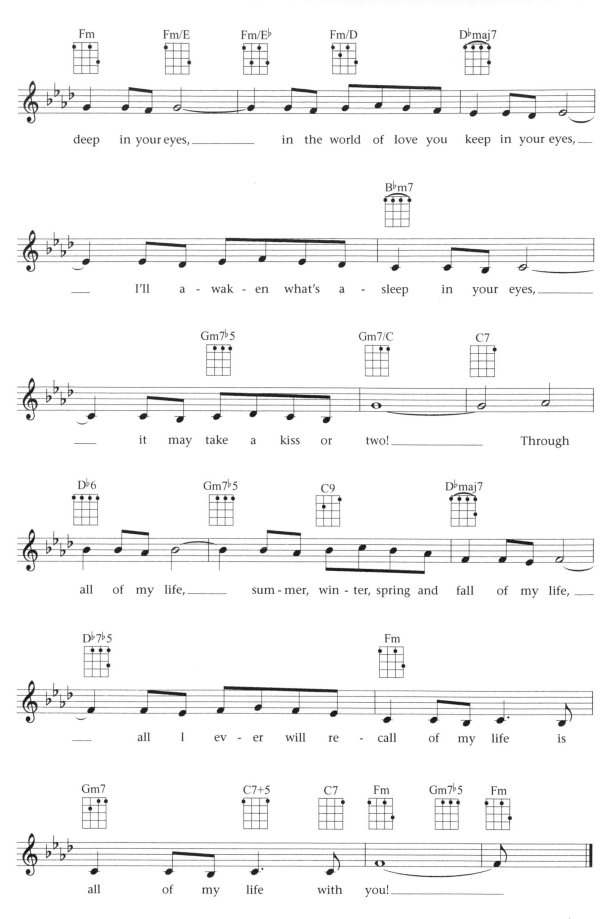

# When You Wish Upon A Star

*Walt Disney's Pinocchio*

Words by
NED WASHINGTON

Music by
LEIGH HARLINE

FIRST NOTE

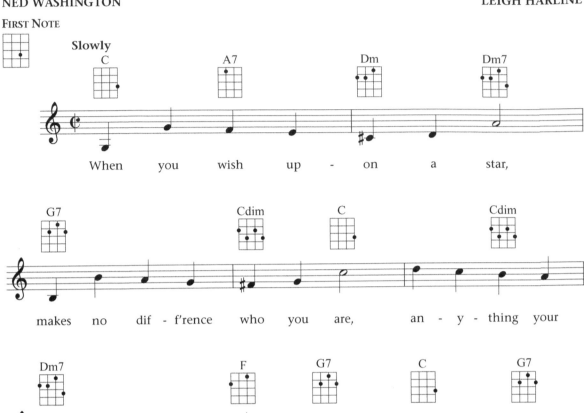

When you wish up - on a star,

makes no dif - f'rence who you are, an - y - thing your

heart de - sires will come to you.

If your heart is in your dream, no re - quest is

too ex - treme, when you wish up - on a star as

© Copyright 1940 by Bourne Co. Copyright Renewed.
This Arrangement © Copyright 2003 by Bourne Co.
All Rights Reserved  International Copyright Secured

# You Made Me Love You

*Broadway Melody Of 1938*

Words by
JOE McCARTHY

Music by
JAMES V. MONACO

**First Note**

**Slowly**

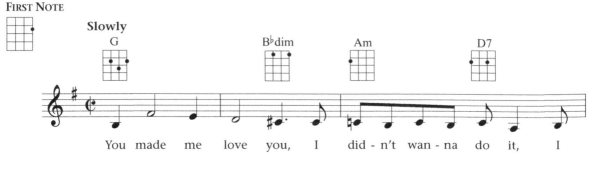

You made me love you, I did-n't wan-na do it, I

did-n't wan-na do it. You made me want you,

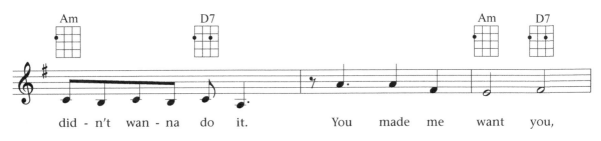

and all the time you knew it, I guess you al-ways knew it.

You made me hap - py some - times, you made me glad. ___

___ But there were times, ___ dear, you made ___

76

© 2003 FLEA MARKET MUSIC
International Copyright Secured  Made In U.S.A. All Rights Reserved

# Young At Heart

## Young At Heart

**Words by**
CAROLYN LEIGH

**Music by**
JOHNNY RICHARDS

© 1954 CHERIO CORPORATION © Renewed CHERIO CORP. and JUNE'S TUNES.
This arrangement © 2003 CHERIO CORP. and JUNE'S TUNES.
All Rights Reserved   Used by Permission

laugh _____ when your dreams _____ fall a - part at the seams and
all _____ you'll de - rive _____ out of

life gets more ex - cit - ing with each pass - ing day, _____ and

love is ei - ther in your heart or on the way. _____ 2. Don't you

be - ing a - live and here is the best part, _____ you have a head-start, _____

if you are a - mong the ver - y young at heart. _____

# Hollywood Ending

**Words by**
**JIM BELOFF**

**Music by**
**HERB OHTA**

FIRST NOTE

Moderately

Gmaj7

1. Hol - ly - wood end - ing, _____ in - to the sun - set, _____
2. Went to the West Coast, _____ Hol - ly - wood dream - ing, _____

E9    Am

boy gets the girl _____ at the end _____ of the day. Good guys are win - ners, _____
look - ing for rich - es, ro - mance _____ and re - nown. Fol - lowed a rain - bow,

Am7♭5    Em7    A7    Am    D7

bad guys are los - ers, _____ want - ed to live my life _____ that way.
found on - ly fools gold, _____ I head - ed back to my _____ home town.

G9    E7♭5 E7 Am    Am7♭5    Em7 E7#5 Am D7(13)

Took my - self to the mov - ies, _____ end - ed up sit - ting next to you. Well...

Gmaj7    E9    Am D7 G

Hol - ly - wood end - ing, _____ in - to the sun - set, it all came true.

© 2003 Flea Market Music, Inc.
International Copyright Secured   Made In U.S.A.   All Rights Reserved